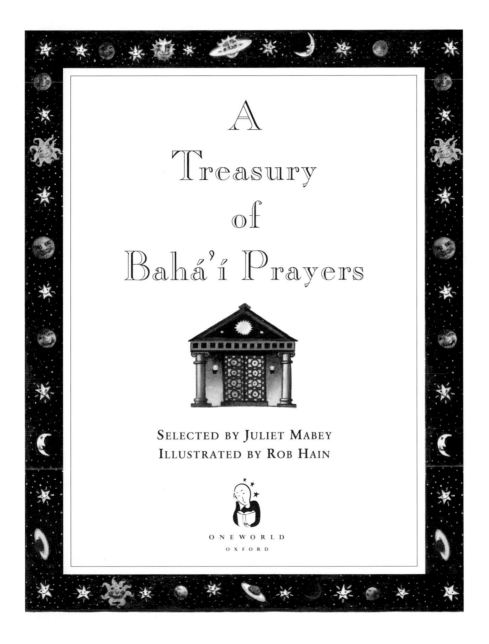

A Treasury of Bahá'í Prayers

SELECTED BY JULIET MABEY

ILLUSTRATED BY ROB HAIN

ONEWORLD

OXFORD

Contents

CONTENTS

4

Assistance & Help

O MY GOD! I ask Thee, by Thy most glorious Name, to aid me in that which will cause the affairs of Thy servants to prosper, and Thy cities to flourish. Thou, indeed, hast power over all things!

— Bahá'u'lláh

O GOD! We are weak; give us strength. We are poor; bestow upon us Thine illimitable treasures. We are sick; grant us Thy divine healing. We are powerless; give us of Thy heavenly power.

O Lord! Make us useful in this world; free us from the condition of self and desire.

O Lord! Make us firm in Thy love and cause us to be loving towards the whole of mankind. Confirm us in service to the world of humanity, so that we may become the servants of Thy servants, that we may love all Thy creatures and become compassionate to all Thy people.

O Lord! Thou art the Almighty! Thou art the Merciful! Thou art the Forgiver! Thou art the Omnipotent!

– *'Abdu'l-Bahá*

My God, my Adored One, my King, my Desire! What tongue can voice my thanks to Thee? I was heedless, Thou didst awaken me. I had turned back from Thee, Thou didst graciously aid me to turn towards Thee. I was as one dead, Thou didst quicken me with the water of life. I was withered, Thou didst revive me with the heavenly stream of Thine utterance which hath flowed forth from the Pen of the All-Merciful.

O Divine Providence! All existence is begotten by Thy bounty; deprive it not of the waters of Thy generosity, neither do Thou withhold it from the ocean of Thy mercy. I beseech Thee to aid and assist me at all times and under all conditions, and seek from the heaven of Thy grace Thine ancient favour. Thou art, in truth, the Lord of bounty, and the Sovereign of the kingdom of eternity.

– Bahá'u'lláh

Evening

O LORD, I have turned my face unto Thy kingdom of oneness and am immersed in the sea of Thy mercy.

O Lord, enlighten my sight by beholding Thy lights in this dark night, and make me happy by the wine of Thy love in this wonderful age.

O Lord, make me hear Thy call,
and open before my face the doors of
Thy heaven, so that I may see the light
of Thy glory and become attracted to
Thy beauty.

Verily, Thou art the Giver, the
Generous, the Merciful, the Forgiving.

—'Abdu'l-Bahá

Hᴏᴡ ᴄᴀɴ I ᴄʜᴏᴏsᴇ ᴛᴏ sʟᴇᴇᴘ, O God, my God, when the eyes of them that long for Thee are wakeful because of their separation from Thee; and how can I lie down to rest whilst the souls of Thy lovers are sore vexed in their remoteness from Thy presence?

I have committed, O my Lord, my spirit and my entire being into the right hand of Thy might and Thy protection, and I lay my head on my pillow through Thy power, and lift it up according to Thy will and Thy

good-pleasure. Thou art, in truth, the Preserver, the Keeper, the Almighty, the Most Powerful.

By Thy might! I ask not, whether sleeping or waking, but that which Thou dost desire. I am Thy servant and in Thy hands. Do Thou graciously aid me to do what will shed forth the fragrance of Thy good-pleasure. This, truly, is my hope and the hope of them that enjoy near access to Thee. Praised be Thou, O Lord of the worlds!

— Bahá'u'lláh

Forgiveness

O MY GOD, O my Lord, O my
Master! I beg Thee to forgive me
for seeking any pleasure save Thy
love, or any comfort except Thy
nearness, or any delight besides Thy
good-pleasure, or any existence
other than communion with Thee.

— The Báb

I BEG THEE TO FORGIVE ME, O my Lord, for every mention but the mention of Thee, and for every praise but the praise of Thee, and for every delight but delight in Thy nearness, and for every pleasure but the pleasure of communion with Thee, and for every joy but the joy of Thy love and of Thy good-pleasure, and for all things pertaining unto me which bear no relationship unto Thee, O Thou Who art the Lord of lords, He Who provideth the means and unlocketh the doors.

— *The Báb*

LAUDED BE THY NAME, O my God and
the God of all things, my Glory and the
Glory of all things, my Desire and the
Desire of all things, my Strength and the
Strength of all things, my King and the
King of all things, my Possessor and the
Possessor of all things, my Aim and the Aim
of all things, my Mover and the Mover of
all things! Suffer me not, I implore Thee, to
be kept back from the ocean of Thy tender
mercies, nor to be far removed from the
shores of nearness to Thee.

Aught else except Thee, O my Lord, profiteth me not, and near access to anyone save Thyself availeth me nothing. I entreat Thee by the plenteousness of Thy riches, whereby Thou didst dispense with all else except Thyself, to number me with such as have set their faces towards Thee, and arisen to serve Thee.

Forgive, then, O my Lord, Thy servants and Thy handmaidens. Thou, truly, art the Ever-Forgiving, the Most Compassionate.

– Bahá'u'lláh

Guidance

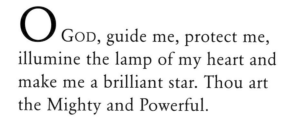

O GOD, guide me, protect me, illumine the lamp of my heart and make me a brilliant star. Thou art the Mighty and Powerful.

– 'Abdu'l-Bahá

Hold Thou my right arm, O God, and dwell continually with me. Guide me to the fountain of Thy knowledge, and encircle me with Thy glory. Set Thine angels on my right hand, and open mine eyes to Thy splendour. Let mine ears harken to Thy melodious tone, and comfort me with Thy presence. For Thou art the strength of my heart, and the trust of my soul, and I desire none other beside Thee.

– Bahá'u'lláh

Healing

THY NAME IS MY HEALING, O my God, and remembrance of Thee is my remedy. Nearness to Thee is my hope, and love for Thee is my companion. Thy mercy to me is my healing and my succour in both this world and the world to come. Thou, verily, art the All-Bountiful, the All-Knowing, the All-Wise.

— *Bahá'u'lláh*

Humanity

O LORD! Enable all the peoples of the earth to gain admittance into the Paradise of Thy Faith, so that no created being may remain beyond the bounds of Thy good-pleasure.

From time immemorial Thou hast been potent to do what pleaseth Thee and transcendent above whatsoever Thou desirest.

— The Báb

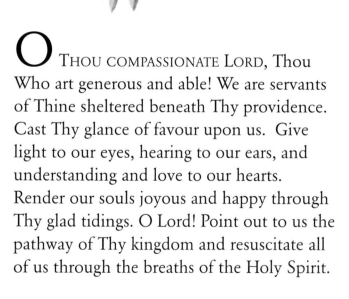

O THOU COMPASSIONATE LORD, Thou Who art generous and able! We are servants of Thine sheltered beneath Thy providence. Cast Thy glance of favour upon us. Give light to our eyes, hearing to our ears, and understanding and love to our hearts. Render our souls joyous and happy through Thy glad tidings. O Lord! Point out to us the pathway of Thy kingdom and resuscitate all of us through the breaths of the Holy Spirit.

Bestow upon us life everlasting and confer upon us never-ending honour. Unify mankind and illumine the world of humanity. May we all follow Thy pathway, long for Thy good-pleasure and seek the mysteries of Thy kingdom. O God! Unite us and connect our hearts with Thy indissoluble bond. Verily, Thou art the Giver, Thou art the Kind One and Thou art the Almighty.

– 'Abdu'l-Bahá

O THOU KIND LORD! Thou hast created all humanity from the same stock. Thou hast decreed that all shall belong to the same household. In Thy Holy Presence they are all Thy servants, and all mankind are sheltered beneath Thy Tabernacle; all have gathered together at Thy Table of Bounty; all are illumined through the light of Thy Providence.

O God! Thou art kind to all, Thou hast provided for all, dost shelter all, conferrest life upon all. Thou hast endowed each and all with talents and faculties, and all are submerged in the Ocean of Thy Mercy.

O Thou kind Lord! Unite all. Let the religions agree and make the nations one, so that they may see each other as one family and the whole earth as one home. May they all live together in perfect harmony.

O God! Raise aloft the banner of the oneness of mankind.

O God! Establish the Most Great Peace.

Cement Thou, O God, the hearts together.

O Thou kind Father, God! Gladden our hearts through the fragrance of Thy love. Brighten our eyes through the Light of Thy Guidance. Delight our ears with the melody of Thy Word, and shelter us all in the Stronghold of Thy Providence.

Thou art the Mighty and Powerful, Thou art the Forgiving and Thou art the One Who overlooketh the shortcomings of all mankind.

— 'Abdu'l-Bahá

Journeys

O GOD, MY GOD! I have set out from my home, holding fast unto the cord of Thy love, and I have committed myself wholly to Thy care and Thy protection. I entreat Thee by Thy power through which Thou didst protect Thy loved ones from the wayward and the perverse, and from every contumacious oppressor, and every wicked doer who hath strayed far from Thee, to keep me safe by Thy bounty and Thy grace. Enable me, then, to return to my home by Thy power and Thy might. Thou art, truly, the Almighty, the Help in Peril, the Self-Subsisting.

– *Bahá'u'lláh*

Meetings

O MY GOD! O MY GOD! Verily, these servants are turning to Thee, supplicating Thy kingdom of mercy. Verily, they are attracted by Thy holiness and set aglow with the fire of Thy love, seeking confirmation from Thy wondrous kingdom, and hoping for attainment in Thy heavenly realm.

Verily, they long for the descent of Thy bestowal, desiring illumination from the Sun of Reality. O Lord! Make them radiant lamps, merciful signs, fruitful trees and shining stars. May they come forth in Thy service and be connected with Thee by the bonds and ties of Thy love, longing for the lights of Thy favour. O Lord! Make them signs of guidance, standards of Thine immortal kingdom, waves of the sea of Thy mercy, mirrors of the light of Thy majesty.

Verily, Thou art the Generous. Verily, Thou art the Merciful. Verily, Thou art the Precious, the Beloved.

–'Abdu'l-Bahá

Morning

I HAVE WAKENED in Thy shelter, O my God, and it becometh him that seeketh that shelter to abide within the Sanctuary of Thy protection and the Stronghold of Thy defence. Illumine my inner being, O my Lord, with the splendours of the Dayspring of Thy Revelation, even as Thou didst illumine my outer being with the morning light of Thy favour.

— *Bahá'u'lláh*

I HAVE RISEN THIS MORNING by Thy grace, O my God, and left my home trusting wholly in Thee, and committing myself to Thy care. Send down, then, upon me, out of the heaven of Thy mercy, a blessing from Thy side, and enable me to return home in safety even as Thou didst enable me to set out under Thy protection with my thoughts fixed steadfastly upon Thee.

There is none other God but Thee, the One, the Incomparable, the All-Knowing, the All-Wise.

— Bahá'u'lláh

Nearness to God

O THOU WHOSE FACE is the object
of my adoration, Whose beauty is my
sanctuary, Whose habitation is my
goal, Whose praise is my hope, Whose
providence is my companion, Whose
love is the cause of my being, Whose
mention is my solace, Whose nearness
is my desire, Whose presence is my
dearest wish and highest aspiration, I
entreat Thee not to withhold from me

the things Thou didst ordain for the
chosen ones among Thy servants.
Supply me, then, with the good of
this world and of the next.

Thou, truly, art the King of all
men. There is no God but Thee, the
Ever-Forgiving, the Most Generous.

— Bahá'u'lláh

I KNOW NOT, O my God, what the Fire is which Thou didst kindle in Thy land. Earth can never cloud its splendour, nor water quench its flame. All the peoples of the world are powerless to resist its force. Great is the blessedness of him that hath drawn nigh unto it, and heard its roaring.

Some, O my God, Thou didst, through Thy strengthening grace, enable to approach it, while others Thou didst keep back by reason of what their hands have wrought in Thy days. Whoso hath hasted towards it and attained unto it hath, in his eagerness to gaze on Thy beauty, yielded his life in Thy path, and ascended unto Thee, wholly

detached from aught else except Thyself.

I beseech Thee, O my Lord, by this Fire which blazeth and rageth in the world of creation, to rend asunder the veils that have hindered me from appearing before the throne of Thy majesty, and from standing at the door of Thy gate. Do Thou ordain for me, O my Lord, every good thing Thou didst send down in Thy Book, and suffer me not to be far removed from the shelter of Thy mercy.

Powerful art Thou to do what pleaseth Thee. Thou art, verily, the All-Powerful, the Most Generous.

– Bahá'u'lláh

Obedience

MAKE FIRM OUR STEPS, O Lord, in Thy path and strengthen Thou our hearts in Thine obedience. Turn our faces towards the beauty of Thy oneness, and gladden our bosoms with the signs of Thy divine unity. Adorn our bodies with the robe of Thy bounty, and remove from our eyes the veil of sinfulness, and give us the chalice of Thy grace; that the essence of all beings may sing Thy praise before the vision of Thy grandeur. Reveal then Thyself, O Lord, by Thy merciful utterance and the mystery of

Thy divine being, that the holy ecstasy of prayer may fill our souls – a prayer that shall rise above words and letters and transcend the murmur of syllables and sounds – that all things may be merged into nothingness before the revelation of Thy splendour.

Lord! These are servants that have remained fast and firm in Thy Covenant and Thy Testament, that have held fast unto the cord of constancy in Thy Cause and clung unto the hem of the robe of Thy grandeur. Assist them, O Lord, with Thy grace, confirm with Thy power and strengthen their loins in obedience to Thee.

Thou art the Pardoner, the Gracious.

– *'Abdu'l-Bahá*

Parents

Blessed is he who remembereth his parents when communing with God.

– *The Báb*

THOU SEEST, O Lord, our suppliant hands lifted up towards the heaven of Thy favour and bounty. Grant that they may be filled with the treasures of Thy munificence and bountiful favours. Forgive us, and our fathers and our mothers, and fulfil whatsoever we have desired from the ocean of Thy grace and Divine generosity. Accept, O Beloved of our hearts, all our works in Thy path. Thou art, verily, the Most Powerful, the Most Exalted, the Incomparable, the One, the Forgiving, the Gracious.

— Bahá'u'lláh

Praise & Thanks

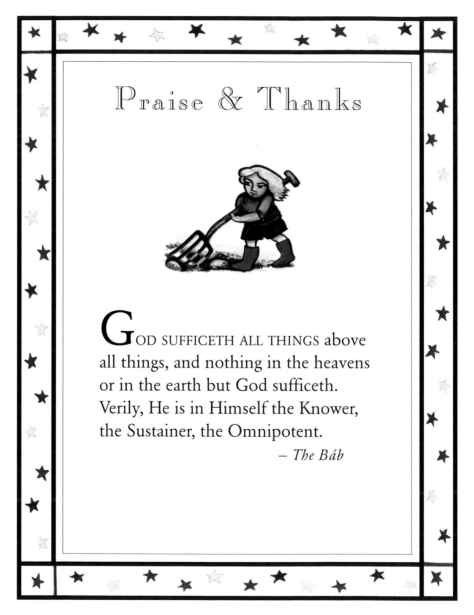

GOD SUFFICETH ALL THINGS above
all things, and nothing in the heavens
or in the earth but God sufficeth.
Verily, He is in Himself the Knower,
the Sustainer, the Omnipotent.

— *The Báb*

O GOD, OUR LORD! We sing Thy praise, bear witness to Thy sanctity and implore fervently the heaven of Thy mercy to make us lights of guidance, stars shining above the horizons of eternal glory amongst mankind, and to teach us a knowledge which proceedeth from Thee. Yá Bahá'u'l-Abhá!

— *'Abdu'l-Bahá*

O COMPASSIONATE GOD! Thanks be to Thee for Thou hast awakened and made me conscious. Thou hast given me a seeing eye and favoured me with a hearing ear, hast led me to Thy kingdom and guided me to Thy path. Thou hast shown me the right way and caused me to enter the ark of deliverance.

O God! Keep me steadfast and make me firm and staunch. Protect me from violent tests and preserve and shelter me in the strongly fortified fortress of Thy Covenant and Testament. Thou art the Powerful. Thou art the Seeing. Thou art the Hearing!

– *'Abdu'l-Bahá*

A<small>LL PRAISE</small>, O <small>MY</small> G<small>OD</small>, be to Thee Who art the Source of all glory and majesty, of greatness and honour, of sovereignty and dominion, of loftiness and grace, of awe and power. Whomsoever Thou willest Thou causest to draw nigh unto the Most Great Ocean, and on whomsoever Thou desirest Thou conferrest the honour of recognizing Thy Most Ancient Name. Of all who are in heaven and on earth, none can withstand the operation of Thy sovereign Will. From all eternity Thou didst rule the entire creation, and Thou wilt continue for evermore to exercise Thy dominion over all

created things. There is none other God but Thee, the Almighty, the Most Exalted, the All-Powerful, the All-Wise.

Illumine, O Lord, the faces of Thy servants, that they may behold Thee; and cleanse their hearts that they may turn unto the court of Thy heavenly favours, and recognize Him Who is the Manifestation of Thy Self and the Dayspring of Thine Essence. Verily, Thou art the Lord of all worlds. There is no God but Thee, the Unconstrained, the All-Subduing.

– Bahá'u'lláh

Protection

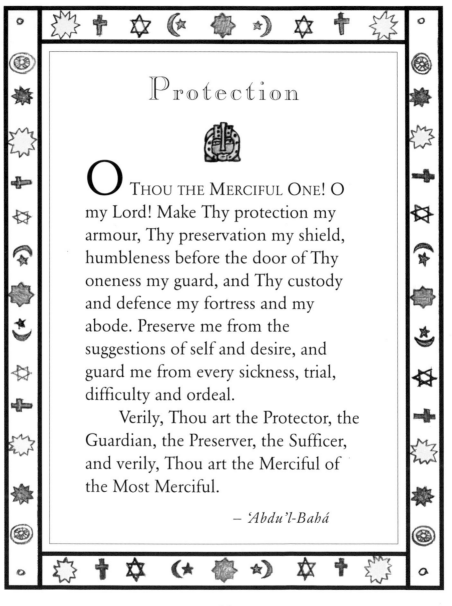

OTHOU THE MERCIFUL ONE! O my Lord! Make Thy protection my armour, Thy preservation my shield, humbleness before the door of Thy oneness my guard, and Thy custody and defence my fortress and my abode. Preserve me from the suggestions of self and desire, and guard me from every sickness, trial, difficulty and ordeal.

Verily, Thou art the Protector, the Guardian, the Preserver, the Sufficer, and verily, Thou art the Merciful of the Most Merciful.

– 'Abdu'l-Bahá

O GOD, MY GOD! Shield Thy trusted servants from the evils of self and passion, protect them with the watchful eye of Thy loving-kindness, from all rancour, hate and envy, shelter them in the impregnable stronghold of Thy care and, safe from the darts of doubtfulness, make them the manifestations of Thy glorious signs, illumine their faces with the effulgent rays shed from the Dayspring of Thy divine unity, gladden their hearts with the verses revealed from Thy holy kingdom, strengthen their loins by Thine all-swaying power that cometh from Thy realm of glory. Thou art the All-Bountiful, the Protector, the Almighty, the Gracious.

— 'Abdu'l-Bahá

Sadness

O Lord! Thou art the Remover of every anguish and the Dispeller of every affliction. Thou art He Who banisheth every sorrow and setteth free every slave, the Redeemer of every soul.

O Lord! Grant deliverance through Thy mercy, and reckon me among such servants of Thine as have gained salvation.

– The Báb

O GOD! Refresh and gladden my spirit. Purify my heart. Illumine my mind. I lay all my affairs in Thy hand. Thou art my Guide and my Refuge. I will no longer be sorrowful and grieved; I will be a happy and joyful being. O God! I will no longer be full of anxiety, nor will I let trouble harass me. I will not dwell on the unpleasant things of life.

O God! Thou art kinder to me than I am to myself. I dedicate myself to Thee, O Lord.

– 'Abdu'l-Bahá

Spiritual Growth

O THOU KIND LORD! I am a little child, exalt me by admitting me to the kingdom. I am earthly, make me heavenly; I am of the world below, let me belong to the realm above; gloomy, suffer me to become radiant; material, make me spiritual, and grant that I may manifest Thine infinite bounties.

Thou art the Powerful, the All-Loving.

– 'Abdu'l-Bahá

O LORD! I am a child; enable me to grow beneath the shadow of Thy loving-kindness. I am a tender plant; cause me to be nurtured through the outpourings of the clouds of Thy bounty. I am a sapling of the garden of love; make me into a fruitful tree.

Thou art the Mighty and the Powerful, and Thou art the All-Loving, the All-Knowing, the All-Seeing.

— *'Abdu'l-Bahá*

I AM, O MY GOD, but a tiny seed which Thou hast sown in the soil of Thy love, and caused to spring forth by the hand of Thy bounty. This seed craveth, therefore, in its inmost being, for the waters of Thy mercy and the living fountain of Thy grace. Send down upon it, from the heaven of Thy loving-kindness, that which will enable it to flourish beneath Thy shadow and within the borders of Thy court. Thou art He Who watereth the hearts of all that have recognized Thee from Thy plenteous stream and the fountain of Thy living waters.

Praised be God, the Lord of the worlds.

– Bahá'u'lláh

O MY LORD! O MY LORD! I am a child of tender years. Nourish me from the breast of Thy mercy, train me in the bosom of Thy love, educate me in the school of Thy guidance and develop me under the shadow of Thy bounty. Deliver me from darkness, make me a brilliant light; free me from unhappiness, make me a flower of the rose garden; suffer me to become a servant of Thy threshold and confer upon me the disposition and nature of the righteous; make me a cause of bounty to the human world and crown my head with the diadem of eternal life.

Verily, Thou art the Powerful, the Mighty, the Seer, the Hearer.

— 'Abdu'l-Bahá

Spiritual Qualities

O GOD, MY GOD! Attire mine head with the crown of justice, and my temple with the ornament of equity. Thou, verily, art the Possessor of all gifts and bounties.

— Bahá'u'lláh

O THOU THE COMPASSIONATE GOD!
Bestow upon me a heart which, like unto a
glass, may be illumined with the light of Thy
love, and confer upon me thoughts which
may change this world into a rose-garden
through the outpourings of heavenly grace.
Thou art the Compassionate, the Merciful.
Thou art the Great Beneficent God!

– *'Abdu'l-Bahá*

O MY LORD! Make Thy beauty to be my food, and Thy presence my drink, and Thy pleasure my hope, and praise of Thee my action, and remembrance of Thee my companion, and the power of Thy sovereignty my succourer, and Thy

habitation my home, and my dwelling-place the seat Thou hast sanctified from the limitations imposed upon them who are shut out as by a veil from Thee.

Thou art, verily, the Almighty, the All-Glorious, the Most Powerful.

–Bahá'u'lláh

CREATE IN ME A PURE HEART, O my God, and renew a tranquil conscience within me, O my Hope! Through the spirit of power confirm Thou me in Thy Cause, O my Best-Beloved, and by the light of Thy glory reveal unto me Thy path, O Thou the Goal of my desire! Through the power of Thy transcendent might lift me up unto the heaven of Thy holiness, O Source of my being, and by the breezes of Thine eternity gladden me, O Thou Who art my God! Let Thine everlasting melodies breathe tranquillity on me, O my Companion, and let the riches of Thine ancient countenance deliver me from all except Thee, O my Master, and let the tidings of the revelation of Thine incorruptible Essence bring me joy, O Thou Who art the most manifest of the manifest and the most hidden of the hidden!

— *Bahá'u'lláh*

From the sweet-scented streams of Thine eternity give me to drink, O my God, and of the fruits of the tree of Thy being enable me to taste, O my Hope! From the crystal springs of Thy love suffer me to quaff, O my Glory, and beneath the shadow of Thine everlasting providence let me abide, O my Light! Within the meadows of Thy nearness, before Thy presence, make me able to roam, O my Beloved, and at the right hand of the throne of Thy mercy, seat me, O

my Desire! From the fragrant breezes of Thy joy let a breath pass over me, O my Goal, and into the heights of the paradise of Thy reality let me gain admission, O my Adored One! To the melodies of the dove of Thy oneness suffer me to hearken, O Resplendent One, and through the spirit of Thy power and Thy might quicken me, O my Provider! In the spirit of Thy love keep me steadfast, O my Succourer, and in the path of Thy good-pleasure set firm my steps, O my Maker! Within the garden of Thine

immortality, before Thy countenance, let me
abide for ever, O Thou Who art merciful
unto me, and upon the seat of Thy glory
stablish me, O Thou Who art my Possessor!
To the heaven of Thy loving-kindness lift me
up, O my Quickener, and unto the Daystar of
Thy guidance lead me, O Thou my Attractor!
Before the revelations of Thine invisible spirit
summon me to be present, O Thou Who art
my Origin and my Highest Wish, and unto
the essence of the fragrance of Thy beauty,
which Thou wilt manifest, cause me to return,
O Thou Who art my God!

Potent art Thou to do what pleaseth
Thee. Thou art, verily, the Most Exalted, the
All-Glorious, the All-Highest.

– Bahá'u'lláh

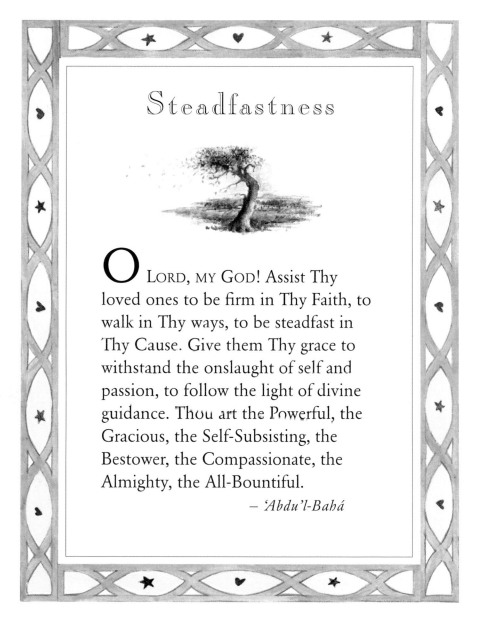

Steadfastness

O LORD, MY GOD! Assist Thy
loved ones to be firm in Thy Faith, to
walk in Thy ways, to be steadfast in
Thy Cause. Give them Thy grace to
withstand the onslaught of self and
passion, to follow the light of divine
guidance. Thou art the Powerful, the
Gracious, the Self-Subsisting, the
Bestower, the Compassionate, the
Almighty, the All-Bountiful.

– *'Abdu'l-Bahá*

O THOU WHOSE NEARNESS is my wish, Whose presence is my hope, Whose remembrance is my desire, Whose court of glory is my goal, Whose abode is my aim, Whose name is my healing, Whose love is the radiance of my heart, Whose service is my highest aspiration! I beseech Thee by Thy Name, through which Thou hast enabled them that have recognized Thee to soar to the sublimest heights of the knowledge of Thee and empowered such as devoutly worship Thee to ascend into the precincts of the court of Thy holy favours, to aid me to turn my face towards Thy face, to fix mine eyes upon Thee, and to speak of Thy glory.

I am the one, O my Lord, who hath forgotten all else but Thee, and turned towards the Dayspring of Thy grace, who hath forsaken all save Thyself in the hope of drawing nigh unto Thy court. Behold me, then, with mine eyes lifted up towards the Seat that shineth with the splendours of the light of Thy Face. Send down, then, upon me, O my Beloved, that which will enable me to be steadfast in Thy Cause, so that the doubts of the infidels may not hinder me from turning towards Thee.

Thou art, verily, the God of Power, the Help in Peril, the All-Glorious, the Almighty.

– Bahá'u'lláh

Teaching

O GOD, MY GOD! Aid Thou Thy
trusted servants to have loving and
tender hearts. Help them to spread,
amongst all the nations of the earth,
the light of guidance that cometh
from the Company on high. Verily,
Thou art the Strong, the Powerful,
the Mighty, the All-Subduing, the

Ever-Giving. Verily, Thou art the
Generous, the Gentle, the Tender,
the Most Bountiful.

— 'Abdu'l-Bahá

O GOD! O GOD! This is a broken-winged bird and his flight is very slow – assist him so that he may fly towards the apex of prosperity and salvation, wing his way with the utmost joy and happiness throughout the illimitable space, raise his melody in Thy Supreme Name in all the regions, exhilarate the ears with this call, and brighten the eyes by beholding the signs of guidance.

O Lord! I am single, alone and lowly. For me there is no support save Thee, no helper except Thee and no sustainer beside Thee. Confirm me in Thy service, assist me with the cohorts of Thy angels, make me victorious in the promotion of Thy Word and suffer me to speak out Thy wisdom amongst Thy creatures. Verily, Thou art the helper of the weak and the defender of the little ones, and verily Thou art the Powerful, the Mighty and the Unconstrained.

– *'Abdu'l-Bahá*

O THOU INCOMPARABLE GOD! O Thou Lord of the Kingdom! These souls are Thy heavenly army. Assist them and, with the cohorts of the Supreme Concourse, make them victorious, so that each one of them may become like unto a regiment and conquer these countries through the love of God and the illumination of divine teachings.

O God! Be Thou their supporter and their helper, and in the wilderness, the mountain, the valley, the forests, the prairies and the seas, be Thou their confidant – so that they may cry out through the power of the Kingdom and the breath of the Holy Spirit.

Verily, Thou art the Powerful, the Mighty and the Omnipotent, and Thou art the Wise, the Hearing and the Seeing.

– 'Abdu'l-Bahá

Tests & Difficulties

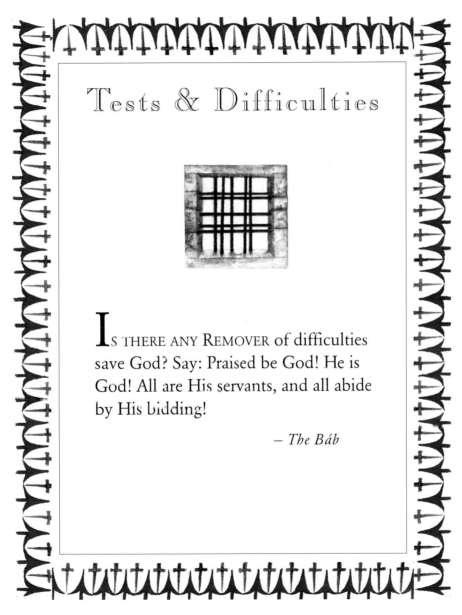

IS THERE ANY REMOVER of difficulties save God? Say: Praised be God! He is God! All are His servants, and all abide by His bidding!

— *The Báb*

I ADJURE THEE BY THY MIGHT, O my God! Let no harm beset me in times of tests, and in moments of heedlessness guide my steps aright through Thine inspiration. Thou art God, potent art Thou to do what Thou desirest. No one can withstand Thy Will or thwart Thy Purpose.

– The Báb

O THOU WHOSE TESTS are a healing medicine to such as are nigh unto Thee, Whose sword is the ardent desire of all them that love Thee, Whose dart is the dearest wish of those hearts that yearn after Thee, Whose decree is the sole hope of them that have recognized Thy truth! I implore Thee, by Thy divine sweetness and by the splendours of the glory of Thy face, to send down upon us from Thy retreats on high that which will enable us to draw nigh unto Thee. Set, then, our feet firm, O my God, in Thy Cause, and enlighten our hearts with the effulgence of Thy knowledge, and illumine our breasts with the brightness of Thy names.

— *Bahá'u'lláh*

Unity

GOD GRANT that the light of unity
may envelop the whole earth, and
that the seal, 'the Kingdom is God's',
may be stamped upon the brow of
all its peoples.

– Bahá'u'lláh

O MY GOD! O MY GOD! Unite the hearts of Thy servants, and reveal to them Thy great purpose. May they follow Thy commandments and abide in Thy law. Help them, O God, in their endeavour, and grant them strength to serve Thee. O God! Leave them not to themselves, but guide their steps by the light of Thy knowledge, and cheer their hearts by Thy love. Verily, Thou art their Helper and their Lord.

– Bahá'u'lláh

Special Prayers

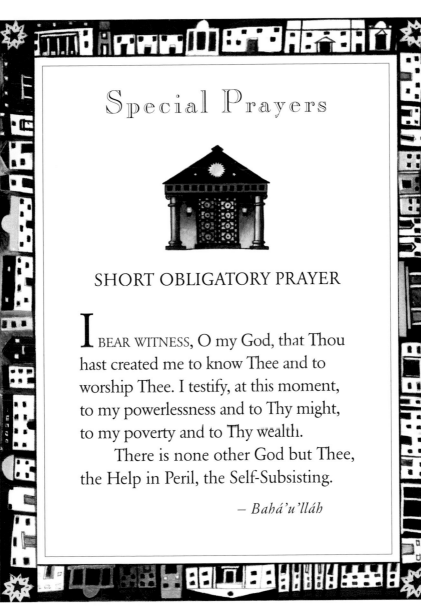

SHORT OBLIGATORY PRAYER

I BEAR WITNESS, O my God, that Thou hast created me to know Thee and to worship Thee. I testify, at this moment, to my powerlessness and to Thy might, to my poverty and to Thy wealth.

There is none other God but Thee, the Help in Peril, the Self-Subsisting.

– Bahá'u'lláh

PRAYER OF VISITATION
OF 'ABDU'L-BAHÁ

This prayer is read at the Shrine of 'Abdu'l-Bahá. It is
also used in private prayer. 'Abdu'l-Bahá says:

*'Whoso reciteth this prayer with lowliness and fervour
will bring gladness and joy to the heart of this servant;
it will be even as meeting Him face to face.'*

HE IS THE ALL-GLORIOUS!

O GOD, MY GOD! Lowly and tearful, I
raise my supplicant hands to Thee and cover
my face in the dust of that Threshold of
Thine, exalted above the knowledge of the

learned, and the praise of all that glorify
Thee. Graciously look upon Thy servant,
humble and lowly at Thy door, with the
glances of the eye of Thy mercy, and immerse
him in the Ocean of Thine eternal grace.

Lord! He is a poor and lowly servant of
Thine, enthralled and imploring Thee, captive
in Thy hand, praying fervently to Thee,
trusting in Thee, in tears before Thy face,
calling to Thee and beseeching Thee, saying:

O Lord, my God! Give me Thy grace to

serve Thy loved ones, strengthen me in my servitude to Thee, illumine my brow with the light of adoration in Thy court of holiness, and of prayer to Thy kingdom of grandeur. Help me to be selfless at the heavenly entrance of Thy gate, and aid me to be detached from all things within Thy holy precincts. Lord! Give me to drink from the chalice of selflessness; with its robe clothe me, and in its ocean immerse me.

Make me as dust in the pathway of Thy loved ones, and grant that I may offer up my soul for the earth ennobled by the footsteps of Thy chosen ones in Thy path, O Lord of Glory in the Highest.

With this prayer doth Thy servant call Thee, at dawntide and in the night-season. Fulfil his heart's desire, O Lord! Illumine his heart, gladden his bosom, kindle his light, that he may serve Thy Cause and Thy servants.

Thou art the Bestower, the Pitiful, the Most Bountiful, the Gracious, the Merciful, the Compassionate.

TABLET OF AHMAD

This Tablet has a very special power if read
when in trouble or difficulty.

HE IS THE KING,
THE ALL-KNOWING, THE WISE!

Lo, THE NIGHTINGALE of Paradise
singeth upon the twigs of the Tree of
Eternity, with holy and sweet melodies,
proclaiming to the sincere ones the glad
tidings of the nearness of God, calling the
believers in the Divine Unity to the court
of the Presence of the Generous One,
informing the severed ones of the message

which hath been revealed by God, the King, the Glorious, the Peerless, guiding the lovers to the seat of sanctity and to this resplendent Beauty.

Verily this is that Most Great Beauty, foretold in the Books of the Messengers, through Whom truth shall be distinguished from error and the wisdom of every command shall be tested. Verily He is the Tree of Life that bringeth forth the fruits of God, the Exalted, the Powerful, the Great.

O Ahmad! Bear thou witness that verily He is God and there is no God but Him, the King, the Protector, the Incomparable, the Omnipotent. And that the One Whom He hath sent forth by the name of 'Alí* was the true One from God, to Whose commands we are all conforming.

Say: O people be obedient to the ordinances of God, which have been enjoined in the Bayán by the Glorious, the Wise One. Verily He is the King of the Messengers and His Book is the Mother Book did ye but know.

Thus doth the Nightingale utter His call unto

*The Báb

you from this prison. He hath but to deliver this clear message. Whosoever desireth, let him turn aside from this counsel and whosoever desireth let him choose the path to his Lord.

O people, if ye deny these verses, by what proof have ye believed in God? Produce it, O assemblage of false ones.

Nay, by the One in Whose hand is my soul, they are not, and never shall be able to do this, even should they combine to assist one another.

O Ahmad! Forget not My bounties while I am absent. Remember My days during thy days, and My distress and banishment in this remote prison. And be thou so steadfast in My love that thy heart shall not waver, even if the swords of the enemies rain blows upon thee and all the heavens

and the earth arise against thee.

Be thou as a flame of fire to My enemies and a river of life eternal to My loved ones, and be not of those who doubt.

And if thou art overtaken by affliction in My path, or degradation for My sake, be not thou troubled thereby.

Rely upon God, thy God and the Lord of thy fathers. For the people are wandering in the paths of delusion, bereft of discernment to see God with their own eyes or hear His Melody with their own ears. Thus have We found them, as thou also dost witness.

Thus have their superstitions become veils between them and their own hearts and kept them from the path of God, the Exalted, the Great.

Be thou assured in thyself that verily, he who turns away from this Beauty hath also turned away from the Messengers of the past and showeth pride towards God from all eternity to all eternity.

Learn well this Tablet, O Aḥmad. Chant it

during thy days and withhold not thyself therefrom. For verily, God hath ordained for the one who chants it, the reward of a hundred martyrs and a service in both worlds. These favours have We bestowed upon thee as a bounty on Our part and a mercy from Our presence, that thou mayest be of those who are grateful.

By God! Should one who is in affliction or grief read this Tablet with absolute sincerity, God will dispel his sadness, solve his difficulties and remove his afflictions.

Verily, He is the Merciful, the Compassionate. Praise be to God, the Lord of all the worlds.

— Bahá'u'lláh

FOR THE DEPARTED

O MY GOD! O Thou forgiver of sins, bestower of gifts, dispeller of afflictions!

Verily, I beseech Thee to forgive the sins of such as have abandoned the physical garment and have ascended to the spiritual world.

O my Lord! Purify them from trespasses, dispel their sorrows, and change their darkness into light. Cause them to enter the garden of happiness, cleanse them with the most pure water, and grant them to behold Thy splendours on the loftiest mount.

– *'Abdu'l-Bahá*

Index

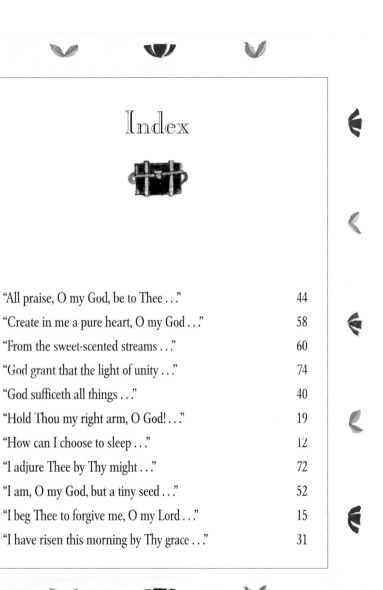

SPECIAL PRAYERS

The headings used in this book have been
chosen to assist in the location of prayers, and do not represent part of the sacred text.

For Shadi, Roshan, Danesh and Bijan

Oneworld Publications
185 Banbury Road
Oxford OX2 7AR, England
www.oneworld-publications.com/bahai

A Treasury of Bahá'í Prayers

A CIP record for this book is available from the
British Library
ISBN 1-85168-019-5
Cover design by Peter Maguire
Printed in Singapore